HAL•LEONARD®

VOL. 77

VIOLIN PLAY-ALONG

AUDIO ACCESS INCLUDED

FAVORITE CHRISTMAS HYMNS

T0066624

PLAYBACK+
Speed • Pitch • Balance • Loop

To access audio visit:
www.halleonard.com/mylibrary

Enter Code
6276-5165-5654-7339

Jon Vriesacker, violin
Audio arrangements by Peter Deneff
Recorded and Produced by Jake Johnson at Paradyme Productions

ISBN 978-1-5400-2926-3

For all works contained herein:
Unauthorized copying, arranging, adapting, recording, Internet posting, public performance,
or other distribution of the music in this publication is an infringement of copyright.
Infringers are liable under the law.

Visit Hal Leonard Online at
www.halleonard.com

Contact Us:
Hal Leonard
7777 West Bluemound Road
Milwaukee, WI 53213
Email: info@halleonard.com

In Europe contact:
Hal Leonard Europe Limited
Distribution Centre, Newmarket Road
Bury St Edmunds, Suffolk, IP33 3YB
Email: info@halleonardeurope.com

In Australia contact:
Hal Leonard Australia Pty. Ltd.
4 Lentara Court
Cheltenham, Victoria, 3192 Australia
Email: info@halleonard.com.au

HAL•LEONARD®

VIOLIN
PLAY-ALONG

AUDIO
ACCESS
INCLUDED

FAVORITE CHRISTMAS HYMNS

Hark! The Herald Angels Sing

Words by Charles Wesley
Altered by George Whitefield
Music by Felix Mendelssohn-Bartholdy
Arranged by William H. Cummings

It Came Upon a Midnight Clear

Words by Edmund H. Sears
Music by Richard S. Willis

O Come, All Ye Faithful

Music by John Francis Wade
Latin Words translated by Frederick Oakeley

O Come, O Come, Emmanuel

Traditional Latin Text
15th Century French Melody
Adapted by Thomas Helmore

O Holy Night

French Words by Placide Cappeau
English Words by John S. Dwight
Music by Adolphe Adam

* cue notes optional

Silent Night

Words by Joseph Mohr
Translated by John F. Young
Music by Franz X. Gruber

11

We Three Kings of Orient Are

Words and Music by John H. Hopkins, Jr.

What Child Is This?

Words by William C. Dix
16th Century English Melody

HAL•LEONARD®
VIOLIN
PLAY-ALONG

AUDIO
ACCESS
INCLUDED

The Violin Play-Along Series®

Play your favorite songs quickly and easily!

Just follow the music, listen to the CD or online audio to hear how the violin should sound, and then play along using the separate backing tracks. The audio files are enhanced so you can adjust the recordings to any tempo without changing pitch!

1. Bluegrass
00842152 ....$14.99

2. Popular Songs
00842153 ....$14.99

3. Classical
00842154 ....$14.99

4. Celtic
00842155 ....$14.99

5. Christmas Carols
00842156 ....$14.99

6. Holiday Hits
00842157 ....$14.99

7. Jazz
00842196 ....$14.99

8. Country Classics
00842230 ....$14.99

9. Country Hits
00842231 ....$14.99

10. Bluegrass Favorites
00842232 ....$14.99

11. Bluegrass Classics
00842233 ....$14.99

12. Wedding Classics
00842324 ....$14.99

13. Wedding Favorites
00842325 ....$14.99

14. Blues Classics
00842427 ....$14.99

15. Stephane Grappelli
00842428 ....$14.99

16. Folk Songs
00842429 ....$14.99

17. Christmas Favorites
00842478 ....$14.99

18. Fiddle Hymns
00842499 ....$14.99

19. Lennon & McCartney
00842564 ....$14.99

20. Irish Tunes
00842565 ....$14.99

21. Andrew Lloyd Webber
00842566 ....$14.99

22. Broadway Hits
00842567 ....$14.99

23. Pirates of the Caribbean
00842625 ....$14.99

24. Rock Classics
00842640 ....$14.99

25. Classical Masterpieces
00842642 ....$14.99

26. Elementary Classics
00842643 ....$14.99

27. Classical Favorites
00842646 ....$14.99

28. Classical Treasures
00842647 ....$14.99

29. Disney Favorites
00842648 ....$14.99

30. Disney Hits
00842649 ....$14.99

31. Movie Themes
00842706 ....$14.99

32. Favorite Christmas Songs
00102110 ....$14.99

33. Hoedown
00102161 ....$14.99

34. Barn Dance
00102568 ....$14.99

35. Lindsey Stirling
00109715 ....$19.99

36. Hot Jazz
00110373 ....$14.99

37. Taylor Swift
00116361 ....$14.99

38. John Williams
00116367 ....$14.99

39. Italian Songs
00116368 ....$14.99

40. Trans-Siberian Orchestra
00119909 ....$19.99

41. Johann Strauss
00121041 ....$14.99

42. Light Classics
00121935 ....$14.99

43. Light Orchestra Pop
00122126 ....$14.99

44. French Songs
00122123 ....$14.99

45. Lindsey Stirling Hits
00123128 ....$19.99

46. Piazzolla Tangos
48022997 ....$16.99

47. Light Masterworks
00124149 ....$14.99

48. Frozen
00126478 ....$14.99

49. Pop/Rock
00130216 ....$14.99

50. Songs for Beginners
00131417 ....$14.99

51. Chart Hits for Beginners
00131418 ....$14.99

52. Celtic Rock
00148756 ....$14.99

53. Rockin' Classics
00148768 ....$14.99

54. Scottish Folksongs
00148779 ....$14.99

55. Wicked
00148780 ....$14.99

56. The Sound of Music
00148782 ....$14.99

57. Movie Music
00150962 ....$14.99

58. The Piano Guys – Wonders
00151837 ....$19.99

59. Worship Favorites
00152534 ....$14.99

60. The Beatles
00155293 ....$14.99

61. Star Wars: The Force Awakens
00157648 ....$14.99

62. Star Wars
00157650 ....$14.99

63. George Gershwin
00159612 ....$14.99

64. Lindsey Stirling Favorites
00159634 ....$19.99

65. Taylor Davis
00190208 ....$19.99

66. Pop Covers
00194642 ....$14.99

67. Love Songs
00211896 ....$14.99

68. Queen
00221964 ....$14.99

69. La La Land
00232247 ....$17.99

70. Metallica
00242929 ....$14.99

71. Andrew Lloyd Webber Hits
00244688 ....$14.99

72. Lindsey Stirling – Selections from Warmer in the Winter
00254923 ....$19.99

74. The Piano Guys – Christmas Together
00262873 ....$19.99

75. Ed Sheeran
00274194 ....$16.99

77. Favorite Christmas Hymns
00278017 ....$14.99

Prices, contents, and availability subject to change without notice.

HAL•LEONARD®

www.halleonard.com